Steam Memories on Shed: 1950's – 1960's

No. 24: London Midland Engine ~~Sheds~~ & their Motive Power

Photographs by **K R PIRT, D DALTON, R HODGE & D H BEECROFT**   *Compiled by* **JOHN HOOPER**

Copyright Book Law Publications 2011
ISBN 978-1-907094-62-0

FOREWORD

The four photographers whose photographs appear in this album all had a passion for the railways, especially the locomotives and the engine sheds. Don Beecroft, David Dalton, Ron Hodge and Keith Pirt travelled far and wide to pursue their own interests in the hobby and luckily we have today reaped the benefits of those travels half a century or more in the past. The newly created London Midland Region covered a vast area of England and Wales at Nationalisation, basically what had been inherited from the LMS without the other vast expanse north of Hadrian's Wall. Eventually regional boundaries were moved and some common sense began to take charge of what seemed to be an unwieldy hotch-potch where old empires ended. From Carlisle to Swansea, Shoeburyness to Bangor and Bristol to Goole, and virtually everywhere in between, the images cover various aspects of the LMR engine sheds and their motive power. The size of the subject under review makes it impossible for an album such as this to cover everything within its pages but there is scope for further compilations of the sheds in future albums. If you still have those old notebooks from 'shed bashes' undertaken long ago, then get them out and read in conjunction with the illustrations and the captions. Enjoy because it will never come back!

Cover Picture (See page 25)

Title Page Picture
The running shed at Wrexham on 2nd August 1955 with N5s dominating the scene. *Ron Hodge.*

Printed and bound by The Amadeus Press, Cleckheaton, West Yorkshire
First published in the United Kingdom by Book Law Publications, 382 Carlton Hill, Nottingham, NG4 1JA

This is 'Scot' No.46112 SHERWOOD FORESTER, minus a nameplate, at Nottingham shed on Sunday 20th May 1962, some four months before its final transfer took it to nearby – but totally 'foreign' – Annesley shed. The engine appears to be out of service and just dumped on one of the coal stack roads opposite the long-redundant coaling stage. Just discernible is the water pipe supplying the top feed is actually disconnected and lying where the nameplate was normally seated on the forward splasher. This engine spent its first twenty-five years of life working from sheds connected to services on the WCML, although during the whole of World War Two it was under the care of both Crewe North and Holyhead sheds on an equal footing, transferring some eight times between those two depots – a human in the same situation may have felt unloved even. Eventually the Welsh shed kept hold of the engine until 1953 when it transferred to the former Midland main line, running out of Holbeck. In December 1959 it finally got to its adopted first home at 16A Nottingham but by then, even after rebuilding, it was run down and due a heavy overhaul. The latter was eventually carried out in May 1960, some three years after its it last Heavy General but there was only so much that could be done to an old engine and after two million miles it was 'tired' and had become, like most of the 'Scots', a bit of a rough rider. In September 1962 it was packed off to Annesley where less arduous work awaited on the Nottingham-Marylebone semi-fasts. Less than eighteen months after starting duty on the old GC main line as one of the 'Annesley Scots' it was condemned in May 1964 and later sold for scrap. Going back to the missing nameplate; it was probably taken off to allow a fitter access to the pipe joint which was situated behind the plate; the other Nottingham 'Scots' at this time still had their plates attached, and did so for some time afterwards. Note the lack of ATC/AWS which was never, apparently, fitted to this locomotive. *David Dalton.* 3

A poorly 'Jubilee' at Nottingham shed in May 1959. No.45656 COCHRANE is dumped 'out of the way' whilst its middle set of coupled wheels are being sorted out either in the fitting shop at 16A or at Crewe works to where they would have been dispatched for serious surgery. The Engine History Card should have this incident recorded although, if so, the details, other than time laid-up, where, and type of repair, would not be indicated. But not having access to said EHC or ERC, I cannot elaborate other than to say that No.45656 got better and carried on working until withdrawn in December 1962. *D.H.Beecroft.*

A busy scene at Nottingham shed on a February afternoon 1960 with 4F No.44248 heading a line which included a BR Standard Cl.4 and two other 4F 0-6-0s. We are positioned on the west facing ramp of the old coaling stage looking at Nos.2 and 3 roundhouses with the 500-ton capacity coaling plant in the background. *D.H.Beecroft.*

In November 1958 Bushbury engine shed was roofless. In a long drawn-out process, its northlight pattern covering had given up after seventy-five years. But the open air situation was only temporary; during 1958 a new roof was added. In the meantime its allocation was virtually unaltered since Nationalisation with a similar number of 6P 4-6-0s at nine, mainly 'Jubilees', and a mixture of LMS Standard type, LNW 0-8-0s and ex Midland 2F 0-6-0s. We are looking at the tender of 'Jub' No.45738 which is topped up ready for the next Euston job but take a closer look through the steam and haze and examine the rear sheet of the tender. Note the elongated holes cut into the top section. Now what was that all about? *D.H.Beecroft.*

Bushbury - 3B, 21C, 2K - Queuing for the ash plant at Bushbury shed, Tuesday, 2nd August 1955 with visiting Stanier Class 5 No.45312 of Patricroft waiting its turn behind two local six-coupled tanks. The original coaling stage has long been redundant since the depot got a mechanical coaling plant and ash plant during the LMS pre-war modernisation programme for engine sheds. The depot closed in April 1965 as 2K, the remains of its allocation joining the throng at nearby Oxley which was, by then, also part of the LMR. *Ron Hodge.*

Crewe North engine shed, August 1951. We are looking across the 70ft turntable pit towards the so-called No.2 (Abyssinia) shed which had been partly dismantled to allow the installation of this articulated turntable shortly after Nationalisation. The turntable was to be the first of two such appliances which would serve two new roundhouses to be built on the site of the No.1 and No.2 straight sheds. This was No.2 turntable for No.2 roundhouse. The other roundhouse, No.1 would have been built adjoining No.2, on its eastern side (segment more like) nearer to the station. In the event, neither roundhouse was built, Nos.1 and 2 straight sheds sufficed to the end and a brick and glass 'part roundhouse' was erected to the right of the photographer, served by this turntable. Crewe North was to have been the ultimate steam locomotive servicing shed with not a thought towards servicing or housing diesels. But those plans were immediate post-war and the shortage of money initially restricted such expensive schemes on BR. By the time the necessary funds were in place the Modernisation Plan had overwhelmed everything connected with steam and so Crewe North made do with what had been provided which was not much in the great scheme - new coaling and ash plants, this turntable and, by 1959, that excuse for a roundhouse. 'Duchess' No.46235 CITY OF BIRMINGHAM appears ready for a southbound working whilst just under cover is brand new 'Britannia' No.70021 MORNING STAR, ready to travel to the Western Region. *David Dalton.*

8

During the period when the electrification was being pushed south along the WCML from Crewe, the Crewe North breakdown crane was regularly used on Sundays to help out with some of the jobs requiring a heavy lift. To get it to the place of work, various locomotives were used including the 5A Pacifics which had, by 1964, become almost redundant. On one particular Sunday in April of that fateful year, No.46254 CITY OF STOKE ON TRENT did the honours and spent the day with the crane somewhere south of Crewe. Great for the overtime but what a comedown for mighty 8P. *D.H.Beecroft.*

What about this then! The ultimate in LMR motive power in the shape of No.46256 SIR WILLIAM A.STANIER FRS. This is Crewe North shed on a Sunday in April 1964 with an immaculate Pacific waiting for work. *D.H.Beecroft.*

A not so clean No.46228 DUCHESS OF RUTLAND, on the same day, on one of those awkward angle stabling roads which were prevalent at Crewe North. Two more Pacifics are to the right, a 'Duchess' and a 'Brit'. *D.H.Beecroft.*

12　**46228 DUCHESS OF RUTLAND from another angle.** *D.H.Beecroft.*

'Britannia' No.70019 LIGHTNING at Crewe North shed in March 1965 with the coaling plant and twin ash plants forming the background. Despite the vast sums spent on the mechanical servicing plant at 5A, it was never going to be enough if the whole of the grandiose scheme was not realised; of course it never was. The outdated layout of the yard combined with the tumble-down state of the ancient sheds promoted nothing but inefficiency no matter how much the staff tried. The place was put out of its misery at the end of May by which time not one LMS Pacific was working and two-thirds of Crewe North's allocation consisted nearly thirty 'Brits'. *Don Beecroft.*

Besides all its various Pacifics, Crewe North shed had a large fleet of 6P/5F 'Jubilee' 4-6-0s. No.45684 JUTLAND was representative of the twenty or so members of the class allocated on 15th March 1959. Note the 'Super D' in the background. These were quite a rarity on the North shed but its presence could be explained by the fact that it had brought a coal train onto the premises. *KRP 209.2.*

A sight for sore eyes? Most would think so. Straight off the works after a Heavy General overhaul (29th March to 18th May 1957), 'Royal Scot' No.46147 THE NORTHAMPTONSHIRE REGIMENT shares a shed road at Crewe South with an unidentified but also ex works 'Jubilee' on Sunday 19th May 1957. The finish is superb and even the Holyhead shed plate has been given a lick of paint. This particular repair was this engine's last Heavy General; the remaining visits to Crewe would be for various casual or intermediate light repairs. Note the roofless shed which was eventually covered but not for a couple of years yet. *David Dalton.*

In June 1958 brand new BR Standard 9F 2-10-0 No.92223 was another ex works locomotive stabled at Crewe South shed, on the same road as 'Scot' No.46147 but outside the 'building'. As can be seen little progress has been made with the re-roofing of the shed, the outline of its original but now erstwhile northlight pattern roof clearly indicated by the saw tooth configuration of the brickwork. Production of the 9Fs was still in full swing at both Crewe and Swindon and although Crewe would turn out the last of the class numerically – 92250 – the honour of building the last steam locomotive for BR was given to Swindon but that was nearly a couple of years away and by then Crewe South shed would have been given a new roof although this section of the shed as not covered over. Also on the ex works line, behind the 9F, is another 9F, No.92043 which had been in to the works for a Light Intermediate repair (5th May to 3rd June 1958) after three and a half years service at both March and Annesley sheds. No.92223 would go to Banbury once it was put into traffic. *D.H.Beecroft.*

In July 1964 'Royal Scot' No.46168 THE GIRL GUIDE was dumped at the back of the roofless (fire damaged and long closed) shed at Preston. Withdrawn in early May, the 7P was still very much intact with name and number plates in place although the connecting rods have been removed to assist a smooth tow to Crewe works where it was to be cut up. Note the patch on the front end of the smokebox just above the deflector - some emergency surgery there to keep it in traffic a little bit longer. The 08 shunter was 'parked' for convenience, as the shed closed officially in 1961. *D.H.Beecroft.*

Remember the so-called 'Austin 7s'? They didn't get much in the way of good press. It was essentially a Derby design which didn't work but the various sheds which were lumbered with them had to make do until something else came along. Luckily, the WD Austerity 2-8-0 came along – in their hundreds – after the end of WW2 and British Railways took advantage of their availability and the bargain price to purchase virtually everyone which had returned from mainland Europe. It was the WD which finally saw off the Fowler 7F although some mutterings were initially heard about the inadequacies of the WD but there weren't many of those and they could at least pull virtually anything using the worst available coal unlike the Fowler engine. This is No.49508 which for some reason managed to survive at Newton Heath until January 1962 as the last of class. Perhaps 26A were keeping hold of the 0-8-0 for old-times sake, who knows! Here on a hazy Sunday 3rd January 1954, the 7F is getting what appears to be a clean! Although the class was by now down to forty-three engines, from 175 just five years previously, it seems strange that No.49508 still had eight years of work in front of it at this time. *KRP .127.*

A real meeting of the regions here. This is Birkenhead – 6C – on Sunday 4th April 1954. LMR and WR types are intermingled in a marriage of convenience. Prior to Nationalisation the GWR and the LMS kept themselves very much apart at this place, each having their own shed, LMS on the left and GWR on the right. It was a bit like Shrewsbury except that the LMR was in charge from Day One. Therefore, the place had some investment, albeit somewhat late in the great scheme of things, in the shape of mechanical coal and ash plants in 1955 (see Western Region volume for an appropriate picture). In the meantime on the stabling roads interaction was encouraged and as can be seen it worked out nicely. Both sheds initially had northlight style roofs (facing south-east!) but the LMS cut back the roof of their shed (ex LNWR) in 1936 and changed it to a multi-pitched style in vogue at the time and shown up here. The GWR did nowt but miraculously their shed roof hung on. Both sheds date from 1878 and both were re-roofed by BR in 1961. The depot of course was one of the last steam sheds to close on BR and its final allocation was probably the greatest gathering of BR Standard 2-10-0s ever assembled. *KRP .188.*

On 27th June 1954, a pair of Nuneaton's G2As, headed by No.49112, stable alongside the shed with another pre-Group veteran in the shape of a Lanky 'A' class, either No.52141, 52429 or 52465; a fourth 'A' class, No.52322, left the shed in September 1952 and returned to Lancashire. Besides the LNW 0-8-0s, of which there were approximately twenty-two allocated to Nuneaton at this time, a number of modern (LMS standard) classes resided to make up a complement of over seventy engines. No.49112 was a relative newcomer to Nuneaton and had arrived in October 1952 from Carnforth via Speke Jct and Warrington. *KRP 6F.8.5.*

A general view of Nuneaton shed on that 27th day of June 1954. Nearly all the types allocated are represented in this photograph; from the left they are a Hughes/Fowler 'Crab', a 'Jinty' 0-6-0, Ivatt Cl.4, Stanier Cl.4 2-6-4T, Stanier Cl.3 2-6-2T, Cl.4F 0-6-0 and the good old 'Super D' or G2A. The only ones not in view are Class 2F 0-6-0, Cl.2P 4-4-0, Ivatt Cl.2MT 2-6-2T, Stanier 'Crab', and Stanier 8F. Considering it is a Sunday, the shed yard is fairly quiet. Situated in the fork of the WCML and the branch to Coventry, Nuneaton was a pure northlight shed in every sense. From small beginnings in 1878, the shed consisted four roads but some ten years later, as the local mining concerns grew, the shed was doubled in size to eight roads. During the next decade further development of the coalfield required more locomotives so the shed was lengthened. As late as 1957 BR saw fit to renew the roof in a style similar to that at Bletchley using old rails which were cut and bolted to make various size trusses, which worked out much cheaper than new steel girders. Besides Bletchley and Nuneaton, a few more LMR sheds (Blackpool, Kirkby-in-Ashfield, Lees) received new roofs during this decade using the 'old rails' method. Obviously, in post-war Britain, which was still semi-starved of new steel profile, someone within BR (LMR) came up with the ingenious idea of using old rails for such purposes as described; a typical backs-against-the-wall idea which saved not only money but precious resource – I wonder if they were ever rewarded. Closure came to Nuneaton engine shed in June 1966. It wasn't required anymore, not even for stabling diesels. *KRP 6F.8.6.* 21

This is the south side of the former Midland roundhouse at Gloucester Barnwood in April 1963 with a line of six-coupled engines stabled alongside. The line includes 4F 0-6-0s, a Class 5 and 'Jubilee' No.45557 NEW BRUNSWICK, the latter a visitor from Burton-on-Trent. By now this shed was part of the Western Region proper and coded 85C; the change took place in 1958 when Barnwood lost its LMR 22B code and was given WR code 85E - it certainly took long enough to ring the changes. It was 'promoted to 85C in 1960 when Hereford (the previous holder of that code) changed to 86C. However, Barnwood kept its LM flavour allocation right to the end in May 1964 and even managed to send some of its 4Fs to the nearby Horton Road shed. *D.H.Beecroft.*

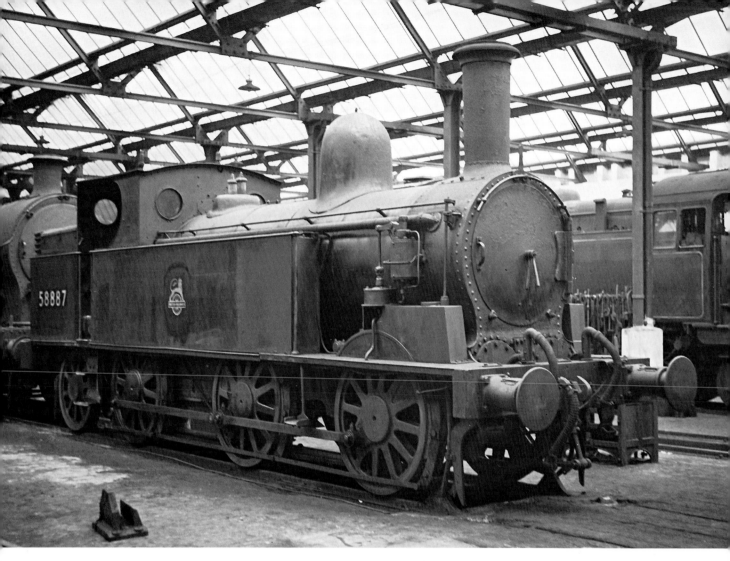

The re-roofing of Bletchley shed in 1954 presented the interior of the building as though it was a paint shop or some newfangled diesel depot full of natural light and little if any pollution. This is the back – office end – and usually the darkest recess of the shed on Sunday 22nd August 1954 shortly after the roof job was completed and the patent glazing was still pristine! The subject of Keith Pirt's picture is of course Webb 'Coal Tank' No.58887 which did not have much of a working life left in front of it so a photograph was necessary before it was hauled off to Crewe and scrapped. Up to this point in time KRP had rarely taken pictures inside running sheds for obvious reasons but this vision must have made his day and the seventy-three years old veteran lived on – at least on film. *KRP 19H.8.1.*

Look at a map of East Lancashire and the town of Accrington falls between Blackburn to its west and Burnley to its east. Each of those towns had been strongholds of the Lancashire & Yorkshire Railway and therefore each had a sizeable engine shed: Lower Darwen serving Blackburn; Rose Grove serving Burnley; whilst plain old Accrington was just Accrington. In LMS days Accrington became the main shed for the District and was coded 24A accordingly, the other two sheds became 'garage depots' and were coded 24D and 24B respectively. There had been a fourth shed just east of Burnley in the town of Colne but it had been closed in September 1936 shortly after it was coded 24C. That latter code lay vacant until Lostock Hall changed from 23E under Bank Hall. Back in Accrington, the shed had all the necessary repair facility requirements for a main depot, besides servicing the running fleet with mechanical coal and ash plants provided in the 30s'. The original northlight roof was also replaced by the early LMS method of providing a single pitched roof, topped with a smoke trough, over each road in the shed. This Sunday 19th September 1954 picture shows that the roof was in constant need of maintenance; such were the corrosive powers of the steam locomotive exhaust, both live and dormant. Entering British Railways, 24A did not have a huge allocation on the books at just thirty-two engines but it was quite cosmopolitan in having LMS Compounds, 2P 4-4-0s, Cl.4 2-6-4Ts, 4F 0-6-0s, Class 5s, 8Fs, and a number of former L&Y engines represented by seven 'A' class, four 0-8-0 goods tender engines, and a solitary 0-6-0 saddletank. Over the following decade the allocation shrank so that by the time of closure in 1961 only ten Cl.4 tanks, eight Cl.5s, two 'Jinties' and two WD 2-8-0s remained to be transferred away to the surrounding garage depots. Accrington then became a diesel multiple unit stabling point for the area. What about Cl.4 No.42634 here, enjoying the late summer sunshine. Well, before moving to Accrington during WW2, the tank had started life working from Newton Heath in September 1938. Four months later it moved on to Bolton. In June 1957, long before the closure of 24A, it transferred to Lostock Hall but in February 1962 it went to Rose Grove. The extremely cold winter of 1962/63 was spent at Carlisle Canal but during the following June it travelled back south, via the Cumbrian coast, as far as Barrow but after a couple of weeks Wigan called and No.42634 moved on to the old L&Y shed there before settling at Springs Branch in April 1964. Withdrawal took place in January 1965. *KRP 22H.8.5.*

Lees engine shed, Sunday 19th September 1954. Contrary to popular belief, it doesn't always rain in Oldham during the summer as this late summer view of the shed testifies. Beneath the original LNWR northlight roof (it was soon to disappear during a BR rebuild) two Ivatt Class 2 tanks share the stabling room with an unidentified and visiting WD 2-8-0. The motor-fitted 2-6-2Ts, Nos.41280 and 41282, had arrived at Lees during August to work the Delph branch in place of the Fowler 'Breadvan' 2-6-2Ts which Lees managed to get rid of to Botanic Gardens shed in Hull of all places. Although eventually a dozen of the WD 'Austerities' were to form the back bone of Lees heavy freight workings, none of the class were allocated on a permanent basis until the end of 1957 however two of them, Nos.90112 and 90626, had spent a fortnight there in 1949 being evaluated. In 1954 the Fowler 7F 0-8-0s constituted the big engines at Lees. *KRP 23H.8.5.*

On a good day Trafford Park shed could yield a plethora of 'namers' - Britannia's, Royal Scots, Jubilees, the occasional Director, and the even less occasional Patriot. In between their appearances the residents were pretty much as presented here - Black 5s, Standard 5s, Fairburn tanks, 3F and 4F 0-6-0s. Of course the LNER side was usually represented by J10s (there is one hiding behind the Black 5), J11s, Thompson O1 and Robinson O4s, many of those looking rather smart whilst undergoing running-in turns from Gorton. WD 2-8-0s too were regulars, especially ex-Gorton works. I remember one day seeing No.90000 and No.90732 – the first and last – stretching their legs after overhaul. Ex works engines apart, Trafford Park was usually full of dirty engines, as here. This scene could have been any shed, circa 1967 but this was 9E and it was 1958! There was nearly always a surprise on shed, the Stanier 5 No.44870 being exactly that – it was from Rugby. The 2-6-4T, No.42064, was one of the local batch used on the CLC lines to Chester and Liverpool. The unidentified Standard 5 is one of the Caprotti examples and has come from a shed with a cleaning regime similar to Trafford Park's; it may well have been one of the Neasden batch. *David Dalton.*

26

Not all of Trafford Park's engines were filthy. Those which had attended main works usually came back looking brand new just like No.42469 here but for how long? Nearly twenty years old when Keith Pirt took its picture at Trafford Park shed on Saturday 18th June 1955 – phew! it was hot too – this Stanier tank had been allocated to 9E since March 1952 having come from Walsall. However, it was no stranger to Manchester having been at Longsight shed from September 1937 to February 1947 albeit working completely different routes and probably never passing Trafford Park once during that time. Matching the Longsight record, Trafford Park kept hold of No.42469 until February 1962 when it was transferred to Heaton Mersey for its last year of work prior to withdrawal in April 1963. Variously coded 19F, 13A, 9E, 17F, and finally 9E again, by British Railways, the shed closed in 1968 with a handful of Stanier Class 5s and a couple of 8F 2-8-0s making up the final complement – all of them were, of course, filthy. *KRP 55F.4.*

Tebay shed – 11C (and other codes over the years) – was best remembered for supplying banking engines to aid northbound trains over the notorious Shap summit. The LMS stationed some of their most versatile and powerful locomotives for the job in the form of the Fowler Cl.4 tanks. BR had little reason to change the status quo and the Fowler 2-6-4T carried on with the job until they were worn out and required replacement by either Stanier or the much younger Fairburn Cl.4 tanks. Fowler No.42403 was far from retirement when it was captured on film on Sunday 14th April 1957 standing on the shed yard at Tebay waiting for the next northbound train. This particular engine started work at 11C in September 1946 and was employed until withdrawal in December 1962. It was not the first time this engine had worked at Tebay as it had arrived there new in September 1933, direct from Derby, but its stay was brief and within a month it was sent to Swansea. In May 1935 it moved to Watford for a short time prior to transfer northwards to Stafford. In June 1940 Stoke got its services for the duration of the war but it left there in June 1946 calling at Oxenholme for a three month stint banking on Grayrigg. The die was then cast and as LMS No.2403 the Cl.4 continued northwards to Tebay and never looked back. The fully enclosed cab gave these engines (Nos.42395 to 42424) an advantage [according to the footplatemen] over the earlier members of the class (Nos.42300 to 42394) which had no windows fitted therefore liable to draught on the upper slopes of Shap for much of the year. Since their introduction in 1927, no less than fifteen of the Fowler 2-6-4 tanks had served Tebay shed, eight of those, such as 42403, had done double stints too. Fourteen of the Stanier and Fairburn types were allocated to Tebay for the same purpose; most of those came and went in the four years from the demise of the Fowler engines at the end of 1962 up to closure of the shed in January 1968. *David Dalton.*

Toton engine shed on Sunday 28th November 1954. Outside No.3 roundhouse which, perhaps being the youngest of the three 18A sheds, at fifty-three years, still retained its original roof. We are looking at the south wall of the shed, specifically at the doorway created circa 1930 to enable a single line of track to run through No.2 and 3 sheds in order to have covered accommodation for up to four of the Garratt locomotives allocated to Toton depot. Considering there was always at least twenty of the class 'on the books' at Toton, providing cover for just four of them seems somewhat parsimonious but not many of BR's engine sheds could or were required to give shelter to all their allocation at any one time. Toton, for instance, had three roundhouse sheds, each of which had twenty-four stabling stalls leading off their respective turntables which equates to seventy-two stalls, each long enough to take a Stanier 8F or two 0-6-0T, say ninety plus locomotives under cover - not bad - on paper. However, Toton had in excess of 160 engines allocated for much of the LMS and early BR eras certainly. So, nearly half were left out in the cold, hypothetically. Take out of the equation a percentage (8%) which would be away at works for overhaul/repair. Then deduct something like 30% or more away at other depots having worked trains out but waiting to work trains back after the weekend. Finally, even though it is a Sunday, some of the allocation would be out on the road doing something. So, all in all their are enough absentees to give the rest some cover except that we have not given any thought to the 'foreign' locomotives away from home and spending the weekend at Toton! Not enough covered accommodation but steam locomotives were hardy creatures and didn't need shelter; after all they spent much of their lives working hard in all weathers over lines exposed to everything the UK weather could throw at them. It was only the men who looked after them who required the shelter. Therefore, the fact that No.47975 has been locked out of the shed at Toton for the weekend need not bother us. Anyway it was dry and fairly sunny, quite a pleasant weekend for November by all accounts. Withdrawn during the following July, No.47975 was cut up at Crewe. *KRP 30H.8.2.*

Inside No.3 roundhouse at Toton shed, July 1956. Behind the saddletank can be seen a couple of BR Standard 9Fs which are stabled on the single road passing through Nos.2 and 3 roundhouse, along their east wall, where the Garratts stabled until the arrival of the first 9Fs in September of the previous year. In the case of No.92064, this particular engine joined the Toton fleet in February last. Before the end of 1958 some thirty-five of the 2-10-0s will have settled at 18A. Although withdrawal of the Garratts had already begun, on this particular day a couple of them were recorded around the shed yard and in steam; No.47981, and fixed bunker No.47998, both being available for traffic. What of the Hasland based 0-4-0ST No.47003. This engine was probably visiting Toton for a repair which could not be handled by Hasland shed; given the circumstances being experienced at 18C, it was prudent to send the 'Pug' to Toton for attention. *KRP 123aF.3.*

Garratt No.47981 alongside the rebuilt No.2 roundhouse at Toton in July 1956. Besides the new brickwork topping off the wall, note the straight line of smoke vents behind the copings. These chimneys mark the position of the through road from No.3 shed. The 2-6-0+0-6-2 seems healthy enough but this particular engine would become one of the thirteen 1956 withdrawals within the class, an event which took place during the following October. *KRP 123aF.7.*

A misfit amongst the Toton allocation in 1956 was ex LTSR 3P 4-4-2T No.41947 which had arrived from Mansfield in February 1956 and hung around for the rest of the decade. What it actually did is unknown to the writer but from numerous observations during its period of residence it did very little. No.41947 had relieved another member of the class, No.41966, which had transferred to Toton from Shoeburyness via Wellingborough in late 1952 but which had been condemned in May 1956. No.41966 had in turn taken the place of another former LTSR 'Atlantic' tank 2P No.41911 which had succumb in November 1952. Besides Toton's little band, two other sheds in the area, Mansfield and Nottingham, also had either the 2P or 3P varieties or both, but in each of those cases more than one at a time. Here in July 1956, in steam, the 4-4-2T just sits along side the water softener doing nothing! *KRP 123aF.8.*

One of the endearing aspects of the steam era on BR was the fact that you could, whilst waiting for a train, while away the time observing the comings and goings of the station pilot or shunting engine. If you were lucky enough you could observe the goings-on at the adjacent locomotive shed such as was available to passengers at Stafford. This is the view of the shed yard at 5C on Saturday 9th June 1962 with a predominately Stanier feel about the place. 8F No.48762 is one of the local lot and is attached to a Fowler tender which did little to enhance their looks and probably spoilt them but that is my opinion and others will have their own. 'Jubilee' No.45585 HYDERABAD is a visitor from Burton-on-Trent and appears impatient to be away. The footplatemen standing by the point are in heavy discussion but the subject of their attention could be anything under the sun. Perhaps the newly 'planted' lineside mast for the overhead catenary is under scrutiny or the overtime to be had whilst working the Sunday engineering specials which were thick and fast on the WCML at this time. Indeed Stafford station itself was subject to rebuilding prior to the introduction of the new electric services and was in the throes of modernisation at this time. Behind the 8F the outline of the Enginemens' Barracks can be made out although just how much custom that place was getting in June 1962 is debatable, its 32 beds no longer required as traffic patterns changed. The shed itself dated from 1861 although the roof was rebuilt at the end of WW2. Closure eventually came to 5C at the end of July 1965 although the shed building stood for some years after BR had vacated the site. *David Dalton.*

33

A few weeks before, on a rather dull Saturday 19th May 1962, Willesden 'Royal Scot' No.46169 THE BOY SCOUT came on shed at Stafford to use the coaling plant and turntable. By now the 'Scot' was ready for the scrapyard, Crewe North having got rid of it to 1A just a month previously. During the year the engine's recorded mileage was just over 27,000, less than half of its 'normal' annual amount. Willesden eventually got rid of the engine in January 1963 to Annesley, in exchange for a 'Britannia'! Annesley managed to nurse another 11,000 miles out of the thirty-three years old 7P using it on the Nottingham-Marylebone semi-fasts. By May the Annesley lads – who were hardy souls – had suffered enough so No.46169 was condemned and sent for scrap. The edifice towering over the engine was built in 1937 as part of the LMS modernisation programme for certain engine sheds or motive power depots as they preferred to title them. *David Dalton.*

'Patriot' Class leader No.45500 PATRIOT was a visitor to Stafford shed on Sunday 15th March 1959. By now based at Willesden, the 'rebuilt' Claughton shows off its coupled wheels with the large bosses, the only part of the original locomotive to survive the rebuilding in 1930. *KRP 212.3.*

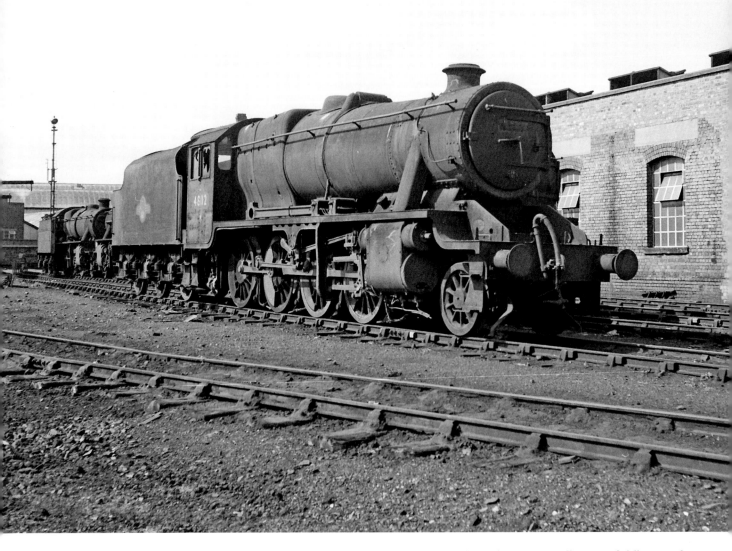

Between the erstwhile barracks and the engine shed at Stafford, out of sight from passing trains, was a small group of sidings used to store the shed's own redundant or withdrawn locomotives but also to stable withdrawn locomotives from other sheds bound for Cashmore's scrapyard at Great Bridge. In May 1966 Stanier 8F No.48112 was one such inhabitant along with Stanier 'Crab' No.42982, seen at the northern end of the siding. The 8F had been withdrawn in November 1965 at Westhouses shed and was en route to Cashmore's. The 2-6-0, which had come from Heaton Mersey where it too had been condemned in November 1965 was also on its way to Cashmore's. A small convoy would be assembled on a regular basis at Stafford and off they would go to Great Bridge and oblivion. *D.H.Beecroft.*

So, how does Kingmoor, as a former Caledonian Railway engine shed, qualify to be a London Midland shed and therefore eligible for inclusion in this album? Easy, from February 1958 the depot was coded 12A under LMR authority and this view captured at some time during the Sixties' gives it plenty of reason for inclusion. Seen on the yard at the north end of the shed, 'Jubilee' No.45563 is by now nameless and without a shed plate, it is also filthy and allocated to Warrington Dallam. AUSTRALIA, as it was once known, was reallocated from Patricroft to Dallam in September 1963 and withdrawn from there in November 1965. The 'Brits' are represented by just one example in this view so we could be looking at summer 1964 or 65, just before or at the start of the great exodus of those Pacifics to Carlisle. The diagonal stripe on the cab side of No.45563 is also another clue and would suggest 1965 when these 'markings' were applied to certain restricted locomotives, rather than entire classes, to stop their use beneath the overhead catenary south of Crewe. On the left we can just make out the number of a visiting Ivatt Class 4, No.43025, which was a Workington engine from January 1957 to its withdrawal in September 1965. Kingmoor lasted into the first day of 1968 as a steam depot, thereafter the code was handed over to a nearby diesel depot on the west side of the WCML and the last bastion of steam in Cumbria was closed. *David Dalton.*

Ryecroft shed in Walsall – 3C – had been extensively rebuilt by British Railways during the three years 1953-55 as can be seen in this circa 1956 view of the completed building. On show are the usual mixture of suburban passenger tank engines and heavy goods tender engines, the latter giving a clue as to the shed's LNWR origin. When built in 1878, the shed contained twelve stabling roads but seventy years later the ravages of both time and neglect presented a building which had virtually none of its original northlight roof intact. Because the allocation was still of sizeable proportions, with sixty or so locomotives housed, BR found it necessary to invest a large sum to give some cover. As a compromise only ten of the dozen roads were eventually covered over but to what avail. By the summer of 1958 the shed had closed to steam and diesel multiple units were housed in the short term only to be ousted themselves prior to demolition of the building. The cost of the rebuilding - it was basically a new shed - seems, with hindsight, to have been a total waste of money but when the authorisation for the expenditure was granted during the early days of BR, the grandiose 1955 BR Modernisation Scheme had not really been hatched. On the left hand road a Bescot based Stanier Cl.4 MT 2-6-4T No.42429 was probably on loan to 3C to supplement the dozen or so Cl.4 tanks already allocated to Walsall in those (just) pre-d.m.u. days. No.42441 in the centre of the picture represents the allocated Stanier tanks; this particular engine arrived here in February 1955 and left at closure in June 1958. Just sticking out of the shed is an Ivatt Cl.2, No.41213, which also arrived in February 1955 but left Walsall in May 1958 for pastures anew at Warrington before eventually moving on to the Southern Region. None of the former LNW 7F 0-8-0 are identifiable but Walsall's fifteen or so at the end of the LMS had been whittled down by closure so that only a couple had to make the short journey on transfer to Bescot. *David Dalton.*

Places such as Mold Junction engine shed were often looked upon as merely depots with nothing more glamorous than a dirty 8F and so it was for the most part. However, many of the inhabitants would be 'cops' to the average spotter on a first visit. A lot of the work done by the motley collection of freight locomotives was away from the public eye and during the hours of darkness. Not so for the Stanier 'Crab' which could be seen working anything from a fitted goods train to an excursion or even double-heading a relief express. As for the Stanier and WD 8Fs, well they were the treasure which once seen, was rarely seen again. Mold Junction entered the BR era with an allocation made up mainly from LMS standard types and a handful of former LNWR engines. By the end of the first decade a dozen or so of the trusted WD 2-8-0s had joined the throng, at the cost of losing the Stanier 8F. Shortly before closure the tables had turned again with the Stanier 8F back in force whilst the WD had disappeared back across the border to England. This scene was captured in August 1955 with both kinds of 8Fs in view with visiting 8F No.48257 from Crewe South. The Stanier 'Crab' was a Mold Junction engine. *KRP 92F.1.*

Shoeburyness – 13D, 33C – Sunday 11th March 1962. Coded 33C since 1949, that remained the case up to closure. Anyway, it looks like a full house at this former Midland outpost in the far reaches of Essex. The days of the steam locomotive are few in this part of the world now that the electrification of the London, Tilbury, Southend line is all but complete. By June the shed and its motive power would no longer be required and the engines will be either towed away in groups or make their own way to other regions (the LMR). The surviving 3-cylinder ex LMS Class 4 tanks (42500 to 42536) were all condemned en masse whilst the other tanks, including a few BR Standard Cl.4, managed to get away to pastures anew and further work - for a short while. *David Dalton.*

A shed bash at Shrewsbury circa 1966. Under Western Region control from 1949, Shrewsbury came back to the LMR in 1963 and was coded 6D until closure in November 1967. In LMS days the depot was coded 4A and from 1949 it became 84G then 89A in 1960. However, Shrewsbury was not simply a victim of regional re-organisation, it was essentially the location of two separate engine sheds owned until 1st January 1948 by two separate companies. Complicated? This view shows the original LMS (LNWR) 1877-built northlight shed which, give them their due, the LMS did nothing to enhance either its efficiency or appearance. The ex GWR shed was to the east (left) of the LMS building and was in an even worse state than this building - that bit looking like a bomb site was part of the WR lot although they had re-roofed their running shed in 1938. So, what went wrong at Shrewsbury? The Western Region likewise did nothing to make the place any better than what it was like when they took complete control in 1949 but they also did absolutely nothing to their own shed either. So a stalemate of sorts had set in and was never resolved during the last eighteen years of the depots 'joint' existence. Petty politics. Pig headedness. Incompetence. It's a wonder anything was done regarding the repair and servicing of the locomotives themselves. As for staff morale? Anyway, getting away from the empire builders and the department promoting a lack of common sense, we will try and decipher what was on shed at this late hour. Ex LMS and BR Standard designs predominate – it is possible that all the former GW engines had gone by now – but they all have one thing in common, the filth! The breakdown crane can be seen to the right of the shed, near to the turntable. *David Dalton.*

41

Regular visitors to Shrewsbury – usually daily – were the LMR Pacifics. They were either on running-in turns after works attention or working in on a filling-in turn. To enable them to turn at Coleham shed, and avoid taking up valuable space turning on the triangle south of the station, a 70ft turntable was installed in 1940. On 30th July 1955, a far from resplendent Camden based No.46257 CITY OF SALFORD has just used the appliance and is ready to work back to Crewe on the next booked train to get into place for a return working to Euston. *Ron Hodge.*

Another LMR engine turned and ready to work home from Shrewsbury on Saturday 30th July 1955 is Rebuilt 'Patriot' No.45536 PRIVATE W.WOOD VC from Longsight which would have worked as far as Shrewsbury with a Manchester (London Road) – Plymouth via Newport express. This view is taken at the north end of the shed yard looking into the Western Region side. The shed pilot appears to be a Fowler 3MT 2-6-2T four of which resided at 84G for much of the 1950s – everyone had a cross to bear! *Ron Hodge.*

It is the penultimate day of May 1959 at Willesden shed and already the depot's Fowler 2-6-2T were being put into storage, pending withdrawal. This is No.40060, one of the push-pull fitted batch which was a relative newcomer to 1A having been transferred in September 1954 from its long time home at Lees (where it was a regular on the Delph branch but was displaced by Ivatt Cl.2 tanks) via Hull Botanic Gardens, Bridlington, Rugby, Rhyl and finally Willesden in July 1957. A long painful journey from coast to coast and pillar to post - unloved, unwanted? Willesden already had a load of these Cl.3 tanks which it could not find suitable work for and had sent away to other sheds. No.40060 was condemned in December and taken away for scrap – unloved and certainly unwanted. *David Dalton.*

The former L&NW shed at Builth Road came under the control of a District Locomotive Superintendent based at Shrewsbury during LMS days. The same DLS had engine sheds at Clee Hill, Coalport, Craven Arms, Knighton, Ludlow, and Trench under his authority. When the LMS side of Shrewsbury shed passed to the control of the WR in 1949 the aforementioned 'small' sheds followed. So, this one-road timber building, dating from 1870, came under WR jurisdiction too. Situated on the western border of Radnorshire, and pretty much on its own for much of the time, Builth Road was one of a number of small sheds scattered the length of the Central Wales line between Craven Arms and Swansea. Shrewsbury supplied the engines which were sub-shedded at this place but by Wednesday 30th March 1955, when this picture was taken, the motive power on shed was an Oswestry based Ivatt Cl.2 which had arrived via the Mid Wales line from Moat Lane to Three Cocks. That line passed beneath the CWL at Builth Road (High Level) and had its own station, Builth Road (Low Level), which had pedestrian and luggage lift connection. To the south of the stations, was a connecting spur linking the two lines and where this engine shed was situated. Normally a 3F 0-6-0 resides in this shed but latterly Shrewsbury had sent one of their 0-8-0s. In 1957 when the even smaller shed at Builth Wells was closed, the motive power from there was sent to Builth Road and so two of these Cl.2 tender engines (supplied by Brecon) resided, each doing pilot duties on the respective high and low level lines. Builth Road engine shed closed on the last day of 1962 but the line it once served is still operational. Also succumbing on 31st December 1962 was the former GWR route – Mid Wales – alas was a victim of the Beeching axe. *David Dalton.*

Staying on the Central Wales route on the 30th March 1955 but going in a southerly direction, we arrive at Llandovery where the LNWR splashed out a bit more on the engine shed there and built this four-road northlight building in 1901 to replace a three-road structure dating from 1868. The LMS took out the westernmost road in 1937 and that is how the shed passed into BR hands. Llandovery was a sub-shed of Swansea (a shed which appeared in the WR shed volume) but this particular shed, via a certain amount of compiler's license, is appearing amongst the London Midland lot (blame BR not me). The main role in life for this shed was to provide banking engines for trains ascending Sugar Loaf summit and these two Stanier 8Fs fit the bill nicely in that respect, although it will be noted, they are from different home addresses. No.48524 was allocated to Shrewsbury (December 1950 to December 1957). It was one of the LNER built 8Fs and started earning a living at Thornton Junction shed in December 1944. In April 1947 it was transferred to the LMS and welcomed at Rose Grove shed for a two year stint. Another two year spell was spent at Aintree before moving south to Salop. This engine appears to have had an affinity with Wales because it transferred to Pontypool Road for a year before moving to Swansea in November 1958. Closure of Paxton Street/Victoria forced a move to Llanelly in August 1959 from where it worked until withdrawn in April 1964. Now, No.48706 had a much faster transition to Wales. It too was ex LNER and it arrived at Aintree from March in December 1947. Three years later, after a round Robin of north-west sheds it was at Swansea Victoria shed from where it worked for the next nine years up and down the Central Wales line and, of course, doing a bit of banking now and again. On the closure of Swansea Victoria, No.48706 moved on to Llanelly too. 46 Llandovery shed remained open until August 1964. *David Dalton.*

Another little sub-shed but of a more substantial construction and from a different origin. This is Tewkesbury, Gloucestershire, a sub of Barnwood, 22B in old money, on Tuesday 17th March 1959. Outside the shed is resident 0-4-4T No.41900 with an Ivatt Cl.4MT alongside the shed. The shed here was opened by the Birmingham & Gloucester Railway in July 1840. That company was swallowed up by the Midland six years later but the shed survived until closure in September 1962 by which time it must have been one of the oldest engine sheds in the country. The motor fitted No.41900 was the first of Mr Stanier's designs for the LMS and was put into traffic in December 1932 at Nottingham. In April 1935 it transferred to Mansfield then exactly a year later it was sent to Bradford where it managed for eleven years before going to Bath in March 1947. After two and a half years at Green Park it moved to Gloucester for the first time in October 1949 but they soon got the measure of it and transferred it to one of the northern outposts of the old MR at Lancaster where it spent much of the time there in storage. In June 1956 an unsuspecting Longsight were given its credentials but they had it in store before the ink was dry on the History Card. During February 1957 No.41900 was ready to be sent to Gloucester but the transfer fell through and it stayed at 9A, in store. The following June Longsight's transfer request was granted and No.41900 moved on to Barnwood from where it was out-stationed to the likes of Tewkesbury. It was not a popular engine from a not so popular class. At some time in 1960 the four-coupled tank was sent to Wellington, Salop, for storage (goodness knows why there) and it slowly rotted until February 1962 when it was once again resurrected for a particular job and sent to Leamington where it was apparently condemned. So the shed behind the malthouse lasted much longer than a Stanier design with more than a touch of Derby influence. *David Dalton.*

The yard outside Longsight's South shed on Wednesday 17th May 1961 with a pleasantly clean resident 'Scot' No.46106 GORDON HIGHLANDER hogging centre stage. Behind is another of the usual 9A suspects, unrebuilt 'Patriot' No.45543 HOME GUARD. The presence of these two engines, along with No.45520 LLANDUDNO, always generated groans from local enthusiasts on regular covert visits to this depot it seemed as though they never worked but as soon as you went lineside one of them would inevitably come along with a London, or a Birmingham express. To the left is Stanier 8F No.48429, a leftover from the days when engines from Longsight moved a lot of freight over the WCML. The DE 0-6-0 shunter is D3767, one of a batch of six (D3765-D3770) which spent most of their lives working from Longsight. Over by the Foreman's office an unidentified eight-coupled LNW tender engine is stabled on one of the four run-through roads awaiting further duty. This particular shed was used for steam, and diesel, repairs and had been rebuilt in 1957 from an eight road to a six road shed with diesel repairs uppermost in the planners' minds. Steam however was not banished from 9A until about 1965 and all three forms of BR motive power could be seen at Longsight in the period 1960 to 1965. Just behind the photographer, out of view towards the right, was a new purpose-built shed for servicing the increasing fleet of 25kV electric locomotives and multiple units. The shed in front of the camera housed steam and diesel locomotives under repair whilst behind this building was the so-called North shed which was the running shed proper where both steam and diesel locomotives were stabled between workings on the main line. Longsight is still an important servicing and repair depot but its appearance has changed somewhat since 1961. *David Dalton.*

Until its transfer to Gorton shed in May 1957, Fowler Cl.4 No.42374 had spent all of its working life in the London area and was variously employed at sheds on the Midland main line, the ECML, the GC main line and the LT&SR line. This rear three-quarter view shows the climbing arrangements for the footplate crew to gain access to the coal bunker and lamp irons on the rear of the bunker. Only one step has been provided beneath the left buffer; a twin set-up on the right does not exist. Once the buffer has been traversed, only one handrail – vertical – is available. The three steps appear inadequate but obviously they sufficed – it could only get better. This location is, apparently, Longsight shed but looking at the robust concrete construction it must be the north shed where light repairs and examinations were carried out. The bigger jobs were taken care of in the south shed where a wheel drop was also to hand. We have no date for this picture but No.42374 was allocated to Edgeley shed from January 1963 until it moved on to Springs Branch in May 1965. So, I'm assuming that the period in question for the photograph must be 1963-64 when 9A would have looked after 9B's charges. *David Dalton.*

The scrap line at Lostock Hall shed in 1967 with Fairburn Cl.4 No.42224 ready for the off. The bunker has been emptied of coal, the conn rods removed and the cab window closed (can somebody tell why withdrawn locomotives nearly always had the cab windows closed?). This 85 tons of prime steel, copper and iron was built at Derby in 1946 and sent to help out on the LTSR line until that line was electrified and all the steam engines made redundant. Most went for scrap, including a couple of BR Standard Cl.4 tanks from that line but the Fairburn engines escaped to the Midland Region. No.42224 went initially to Stoke in June 1962 then, some three years later, to Chester for a few weeks prior to moving on to Fleetwood. At neither place was its services really required. The same can be said for Lostock Hall which acquired the tank in February 1966 and condemned it in January 1967. In front of the Cl.4 is Standard Cl.2 No.78041 which was withdrawn in May 1967 when only thirteen years old. It was a tough old time for steam. *David Dalton.*

The Ivatt Cl.4 2-6-0s always appeared as though something was missing; as though they were more austere than the WD Austerity 2-8-0s. That is certainly the case with No.43046 stabled outside the shed at Lostock Hall circa 1967 with Kingmoor 'Brit' No.70032 TENNYSON for company. Although the Class 4 arrived at Lostock Hall in February 1966, it had not yet acquired a shed plate so more than likely it never got one anyway. Lostock Hall was of course one of the depots involved with the last day of steam working on British Railways but these two would not be around for that event in August 1968: No.43046 was condemned in November 1967. No.70032 went somewhat earlier on the last day of September 1967. *David Dalton.*

It is early on a Sunday morning in April 1968. The sun is shining brightly the 'shed bashers' are out in force, the end of steam is but months away and only a few sheds in the north-west are still operational. This is Edge Hill - one of the few - but only a few weeks away from closure. We are looking at the twelve road shed which faced the east and was erected in 1901 to compliment the twenty-road building behind which faced westward - six roads continued through from this shed into the larger one to enable run through. The original northlight roof on this building was replaced by the LMS prior to the outbreak of WW2, the style used being very similar to the new 10-road shed at Royston in Yorkshire which was opened by the LMS in 1932. The style was subsequently used on many LMS shed rebuilds during the pre-war years at places such as Accrington, Bacup, Barrow, Birkenhead, Carstairs, Edgeley, Farnley Junction, Huddersfield, Mirfield, Newton Heath, Oxenholme, Perth, Southport, and Watford. However, that style was itself superseded by a more durable design using pre-cast concrete beams and standard size roof components which was also adopted by British Railways. Back at 8A the clock is ticking. All the elements of low morale and overall neglect are in place with wall-to-wall dirty locomotives and a general feeling of gloom, despite the sun. Edge Hill closed to steam on 6th May 1968 but a small purpose-built diesel depot kept the famous name going until it too closed in 1986. *David Dalton.*

The former Midland Railway roundhouse at Spital Bridge, Peterborough became Eastern Region property in 1950 and was coded 35C. Up to that time, it had enjoyed being 16B and subordinate to Nottingham, some distance away to the north-west. The shed was a typical second generation square roundhouse with three roof pitches supported by deep lattice girders on cast iron columns positioned around the turntable. Opened in 1872, it still displayed the ornamental brickwork associated with the first generation square roundhouses which was missing from the later built roundhouses. When the ER took over, the allocation was very much of a LMR flavour with nothing but Derby produced locomotives all over the depot: 2P and 4P 4-4-0, 3F and 4F 0-6-0, and 3F 0-6-0T. In 1959, just before closure, the Derby influence had waned slightly but was still present in the form of a clutch of ex LT&SR 4-4-2Ts, a dozen 4Fs, and a number of LNER locomotives including B1, D16 and J39 types, along with a handful of WD 2-8-0s. This view of the shed yard circa July 1956 reveals B12 No.61565, one of five allocated to Spital Bridge, a visiting 'Super D', and Fairburn 2-6-4T No.42061 from Rugby. Closed on the first day of February 1960, the shed and the mechanical coaling plant were afterwards demolished. What was left of the allocation was dispersed. *David Dalton.*

The 'old' shed at Patricroft at an unknown date in 1967. The BR Standard Cl.5s fitted with Caprotti valve gear became something of a fixture at this shed - the exact numbers allocated are not known but upwards of thirty resided here in the final years of the shed's life. Of course, an equal number of conventional Stanier Cl.5s were also shedded here but strangely none of the Caprotti versions were amongst those. The shed we are viewing here was built in 1885 and was originally somewhat longer than building depicted here; subsequent rebuilding by both the LMS and BR being responsible for he reduction. Its younger, and larger, counterpart – ten roads wide – dated from 1904 was situated behind the water tank on the right, and at right-angles to this building, virtually facing south-east whereas this shed faced south-west. The 1904 shed was a replacement for another shed situated nearer to Manchester at Ordsall Lane. Not quite making it to the end of steam, Patricroft closed on 1st July 1968 when most of the engines still resident were condemned. Although filth is the livery of the day amongst all the engines in the picture, only two are identifiable, both Stanier Cl.5s and both visitors: second from right is No.45259 from Kingmoor and next to that is No.45436 from Birkenhead. *David Dalton.*

Kingmoor engines were regular daily visitors to Patricroft shed and in August 1967 a by now nameless 'Britannia' No.70023 is going through the servicing routine over the ashpit at 9H nee 26F. The coal and ash plants at Patricroft completed the third, long side (hypotenuse), of the triangular layout of the depot. It appeared to work, with few drawbacks although the fact that Patricroft had two entrance/exits must have been a plus. Note that the Pacific appears to have a non-standard numberplate, the original being taken off at the same time as the nameplates perhaps - for safe keeping? Considering their longevity towards the end of steam on BR, when compared with the 'Scots' and LMS Pacifics, a number of the 'Brits' were strangely never fitted with ATC/AWS; No.70023 was one of them. *D.H.Beecroft.* 55

Even though Wrexham Rhosddu shed had its origins steeped in one of the constituents of the LNER, it became part of the LMR in 1949 and was coded 6E under Chester. But that was not going to last because in 1958 the Western Region claimed it and the shed was re-coded 84K. But having two engine sheds in the same town brought the WR to the conclusion that one was going to have to go. Croes Newydd won the day, after all loyalties were bound to lie with a former GWR depot. So, in early January 1960 Rhosddu was closed and by which time its allocation had changed somewhat from near ex LNER in 1950 to fifty percent ex GWR at closure with not one former LNER type within twenty miles. Opened in 1912 by the Great Central, and being so far away from the parent system, the six road shed was virtually self contained and could carry out heavy repairs, including boiler changes to any of its engines. This undated view was taken circa 1959 and the engines on view include two BR Std. Cl.3, Nos.82031 and 82037, An Ivatt Cl.2 tank, No.41285, and 'Pannier' No.1669. *David Dalton.*

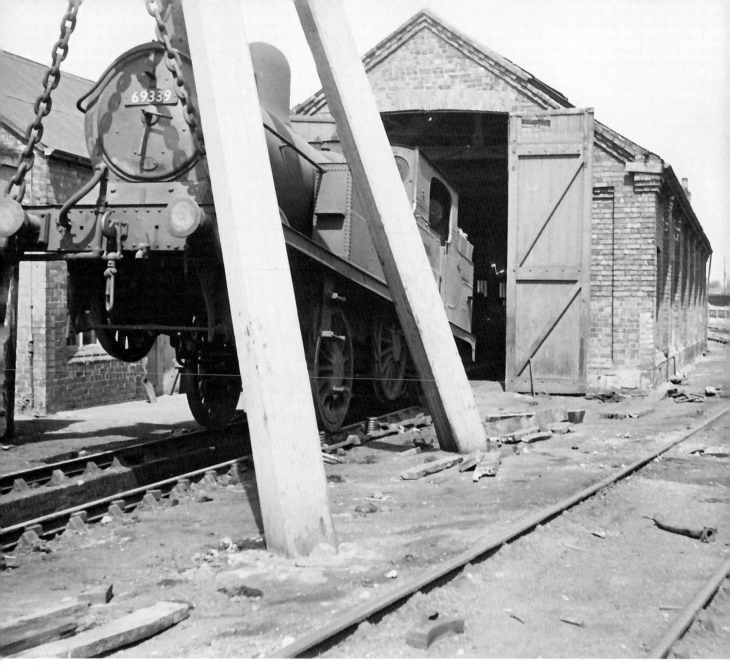

The repair shop and its shearlegs at Wrexham, 2nd August 1955. As already mentioned, this place was quite self-contained and could look after its own allocation without too much fuss. This is N5 No.69339 in a somewhat compromising situation beneath the shearlegs which were situated on the north-west corner of the site, the engine shed standing to the right of the photographer. The N5 was eventually required to visit Gorton where in March 1956 it was condemned. *Ron Hodge.*

Its funny how old boundaries take such a long time to disappear. Decades after the demise of the Lancashire & Yorkshire Railway, Goole engine shed could still muster a respectable number of former LYR engines in July 1955. Amongst them was this tiny 0-4-0 saddletank which was used almost exclusively for shunting and trip working on the nearby docks. Besides No.51222 being on shed this Sunday, No.51240 was tucked away inside the roofless 'shed' at the back. Two other Aspinall 0-4-0STs also resided here at this time – Nos.51241 and 51244 – along with a batch of 0-6-0ST comprising, in July 1955, Nos.51323, 51361, 51432, 51503, 51516, 51521, eight 0-6-0 'A' class tender engines finished off the L&Y lot. As well as the pre-Grouping classes, ex LMS 2-6-0s and 2-6-4T, along with numerous WD 2-8-0s completed the allocation. The shed itself was in the middle of a rebuilding programme which had been going on for some time and would not be complete until November 1955. Having been coded 25C since the mid-1930s, Goole became part of the North Eastern Region in 1956 becoming initially 53E under Hull Dairycoates then, in 1960, under York it became 50D and was one of the last steam depots in the Region. *Ron Hodge.*

A line of ancient ex Midland 2F 0-6-0s extend out of the rear entrance at Canklow shed – 19C – on Sunday 17th July 1955. You could be forgiven for thinking this was a batch of stored or even withdrawn engines waiting for the last journey to Derby but No.58238 is being fired up for the Monday morning work it is earmarked to perform. The others have yet to be got ready. Except for the numbers and a little bit of rebuilding, this same lot of engines could have been lined-up here on a Sunday if you could go back in time to 1885 or earlier – old habits. Although a mechanical coaling plant was not one of the assets at this depot, the road crane has obviously been used recently to clear the coal stacks on either side of the extended stabling road – much of the coal being delivered straight into the 2F tenders it seems. The other 0-6-0s in the line comprise Nos.58114, 58170 and nearest the camera 58204. Canklow passed into the Eastern Region in 1958, becoming 41E, but its qualifications for inclusion in this album are impeccable. *David Dalton.*

Most locomotives attending Horwich works for overhaul would be taken to Bolton shed afterwards for running-in prior to their return home. On Sunday 18th March 1962, Ivatt Cl.4 No.43027 was in steam at Bolton after arriving from Horwich during the previous week. Its home shed was Kingmoor and it would be heading to Carlisle on a revenue earning journey by mid week. In October 1964 the 2-6-0 moved south to Carnforth then, in April 1967, to Workington. Finally, in January 1968 it transferred to Lostock Hall where it was withdrawn in May. *David Dalton.*

It wasn't very often that a photographer could get four locomotives all allocated to the same shed in the same view, with numbers showing. However, on 4th August 1955 Ron Hodge managed to do such a feat at Llandudno Junction shed without too much effort. From left to right (with relevant arriving and departing dates) we have Caprotti Class 5 No.44739 (July 1948, new to November 1963), Stanier Cl.3MT No.40123 (March 1947 to October 1961 withdrawal), Ivatt Cl.2 No.41236 – just two digits out on that last figure to make a nice run (July 1952 to May 1957)! Finally, BR Standard Cl.4 No.75030 (February 1955 to December 1956) fills the right side of the frame. As usual during this period of BR locomotive history, all four have something in common - filth! The shed roof at 6G was in dire need of replacement and that project was begun shortly after this scene was captured on film. *Ron Hodge.*

Chester Northgate, 2nd August 1955. So, why are we at this former Great Central/LNER engine shed in the heart of Cheshire? Because it became part of the London Midland Region proper in 1949 and was coded 6D. Although its allocation then was essentially ex GCR in flavour with half a dozen C13 tank engines, a couple of J10 tender engines and a similar number of N5s, along with visiting J11, O4 and O1 from Gorton, the shed was part of the LMR 6 district. Within that same district was, indeed within the same town, was the former LNWR shed which became the top shed and was coded 6A but nearby was the former Great Western shed which also came under the authority of 6A. Quite a cosmopolitan situation whereby everybody kept hold of what they knew best for a long as possible before the inevitable regional standardisation took effect. Keeping hold of its past for as long as possible, 6D had J10 No.65140 on its books in 1955 and intended it to stay that way. No.65140 is stabled just off the turntable virtually within throwing distance of the LMR main line to North Wales which was a lower elevation and therefore out of sight beyond the small shed behind the J10. Dating from 1874, the engine shed here consisted two roads and was built by the Manchester, Sheffield & Lincolnshire Railway. In 1950 it was rebuilt when the original pitched roof was replaced in the LMS lourve style, using concrete as the main medium. Closure took place in 1960 but by then the allocation consisted BR Standard and ex LMS types. Whatever happened to that grounded coach body alongside the engine shed? *Ron Hodge.*

Chester Northgate shed – 6D – on 2nd August 1955 with Wrexham based N5 No.69362 alongside the half-ton capacity semi-mechanical coaling plant. Now these particular plants didn't take the back breaking work out of the coaling process at engine sheds like the huge concrete towers serving many of the larger depots but they did eliminate the manual elevation of numerous shovelfuls of coal. The tiny skips running on their own miniature railway still had to be filled by hand from the standard gauge wagons before being positioned over the below-ground coaling skip and tipped. How many of those wheeled skips were required to fill the half ton skip is unknown but the railway technical press of the 1930s will no doubt have the answer. Just coming into frame on the right is the canopy of the open shed covering the coal wagons. The LNER were certainly generous to the coalmen at Chester in their quest for further efficiency. Anyway, for the modellers amongst you - what a superb model railway project this would be to enhance a small engine shed such as the Northgate layout where the ex Great Central engine shed had two covered roads and a small allocation. *Ron Hodge.*

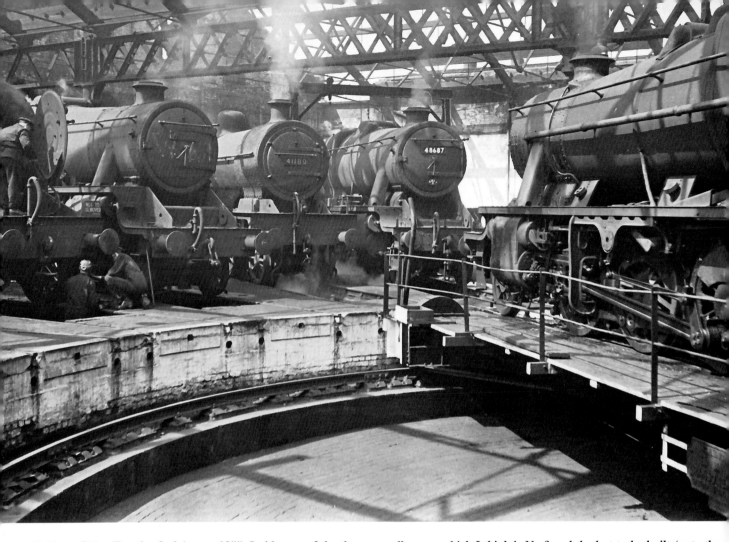

Saltley – 21A – Tuesday 2nd August 1955. Inside one of the three roundhouses, which I think is No.3 and the last to be built (note the lattice pattern main girders) but I do stand to be corrected. By this date in 1955 this particular shed was in need of a new roof and that is exactly what it got – eventually. All of the Saltley roundhouses were re-roofed by BR over an eight year period from 1948 to 1956. Having no roof over its head never did bother a steam locomotive, they did after all spend most of their time out on the road but, shed staff took exception to getting wet especially whilst carrying out an awkward, heavy, dirty job which was usually the case with steam engines. The three lads working on what appears to be a 'Crab' don't seem too bothered about a lack of roof today but it is summertime and yes the sun is shining. Anyway, a nice little scene is presented to us here with an unidentified Stanier 8F on the turntable whilst sister No.48687, a 21A resident, sits in its stall. Next to that is 4P 4-4-0 No.41180 which is a recent(ish) arrival – September 1951 – from the Scottish Region. Its transfer to Saltley basically guaranteed that it was not going to be broken up at Kilmarnock works when condemned; unlike its compatriots stuck north of the border which mostly ended up being dispatched at Kilmarnock. Derby was the venue for No.41180's demise. The Stanier 5 smokebox numberplate is unidentifiable, likewise the shed plate, but it has worked in from the Western Division, assuming the chalked legend is W637 or W657. *Ron Hodge.*

Saltley yard with a pair of 'Crabs', Nos.42791 and 42930 over the ash pits, 2nd August 1955. An 8F is doing the coaling plant. *Ron Hodge.*

A panoramic vista of Derby engine shed on Friday 5th August 1955 with ex works Johnson 1P 0-4-4T No.58065 trying to obscure the view. The twin roundhouses at this place were the culmination of various other engine sheds – mainly roundhouses in the true sense – which had been established here by the constituent components of the Midland Railway. Built in 1890, this particular shed served steam locomotion until March 1967 when closure intervened; afterwards they were demolished. Ironically, the roundhouses which they replaced survived as part of the locomotive works complex and were still in use as stores long after the demise of the square twin roundhouses. Facilitated as it was with the locomotive works, and standing abreast various major junctions, it was obvious that stabling room within the engine shed here was never going to satisfy requirements so an outside turntable with numerous radiating roads – basically a roundhouse without a building – was created on the south-east corner of the shed thereby offering stabling room, albeit uncovered, for locomotives. Visible from this angle, six lines of stabling tracks were laid down alongside the north wall of the shed but even this area would become choked at certain weekends. A similar situation existed on the south wall side. Ex works engines especially were stabled outside pending their local running-in turns and it became a favourite place for photographers at certain times of the day when the near sparkling black paintwork – like 58065's – gave them a refreshing appearance. *Ron Hodge.*

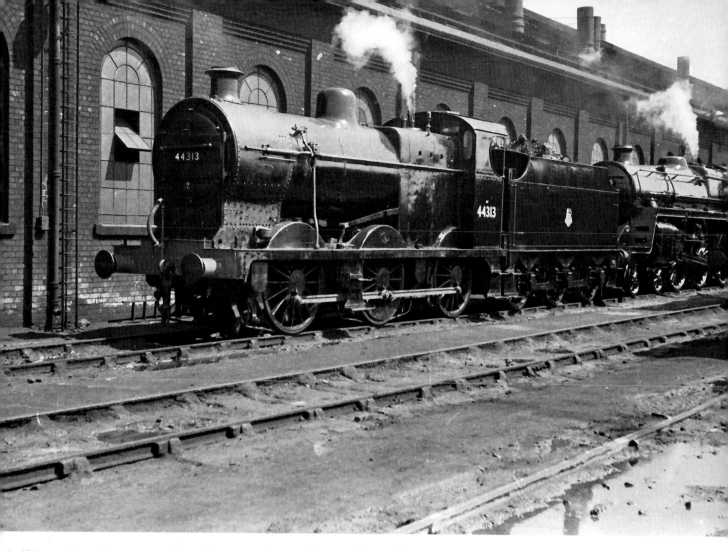

As if by magic we have managed to conjure up a picture taken at said spot alongside the twin roundhouse. It is still Friday 5th August 1955 and ex shops are Nottingham based 4F No.44313 which turned out to be one of the early casualties of the class, being withdrawn in December 1959; this may well have been its last visit to works for overhaul. Behind the 0-6-0 is newly delivered BR Standard Class 5 No.73085 which was about to embark on a career working on the Southern Region where it would enjoy a somewhat longer working life than most of its contemporaries sent to other regions. Another ex works engine on the shed yard that day was Fowler Cl.3 No.40070 from Carnforth, and the aforementioned 1P which normally resided at Plaistow but being push-pull fitted was soon to move to Newark to work out its remaining days – years as it worked out – on the Southwell branch. *Ron Hodge.*

Devons Road, Bow, 24th September 1955 – before the diesels arrived en masse. The former North London Railway depot once comprised two similar sized, northlight pattern, engine sheds both of which opened in 1882. The shed on the east side of the site was closed by the LMS and afterwards demolished whilst the other shed was rebuilt in 1946 using the concrete 'louvre' style which was popular during this period. In 1958 steam was banished from the shed, the allocation being dispersed between March and June, and after a further rebuilding the shed re-opened as BR's first purpose built diesel depot albeit a retro installation. However, enough experience was gained during its use to enable BR to built new sheds for the sole purpose of servicing diesel locomotives. Devons Road closed in 1964 and its small allocation of diesel locomotives, mainly English Electric Type 1 Bo-Bos and a number of other designs moved to Stratford. In this view we see 4F No.44441, a 1D resident until March 1958, in the company of Ivatt Cl.4 2-6-0s of which Devons Road had six up to closure, but the majority of the allocation was made up of about forty LMS 3F 'Jinty' 0-6-0 tank engines which worked the local yards and trips in the area. The massive water tank which dominated the south perimeter of the depot is by now dwarfed itself by high-rise residential accommodation. *Ron Hodge.*

One of the aforementioned 'Jinties' No.47310 outside a strangely quiet shed on Saturday afternoon, 24th September 1955. Like the rest of British Railways, Devons Road was finding it difficult to recruit footplate staff that started their career as cleaners before work on the footplate proper. *Ron Hodge.*

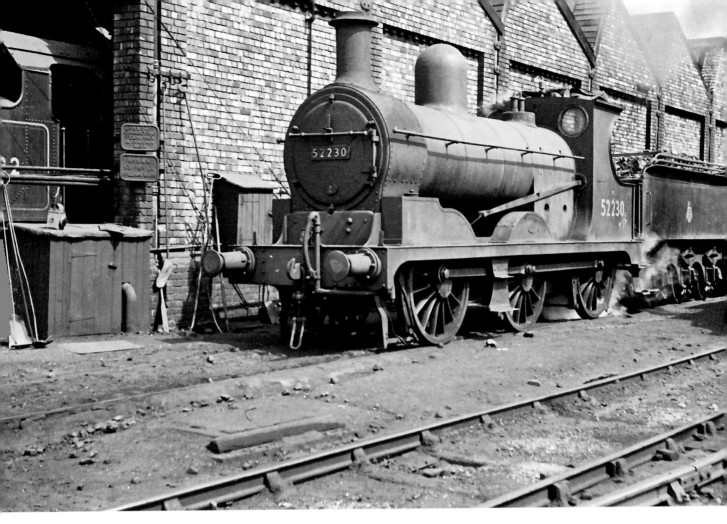

Bangor shed – 6H – Thursday 4th August 1955 with ex Lanky 'A' class No.52230 stabled alongside the northlight shed. A long time resident of Bangor, the 0-6-0 returned to its native patch in June 1958, firstly to Wigan then onto Newton Heath where at age sixty-seven it was withdrawn in 1961. Although found in all corners of the former Lancashire & Yorkshire system, the 'A' class got to the most unlikeliest of places during LMS and latterly BR days. Bangor was just one of the places where they worked for many years. It would be interesting to know the opinion of footplatemen from places other than those sheds on the old L&YR as to their experience with these versatile 0-6-0s. Bangor had at least four of the class in BR days, Rhyl likewise, Birkenhead, Moor Row, Shrewsbury, Workington, Sutton Oak, Nuneaton, Speke Junction, Edge Hill, Royston, and even Hereford all had one or more examples for some years but perhaps the most surprising home was the locomotive works at Crewe where a dozen or so worked the yards. Most of those moved back to Lancashire sheds afterwards to continue working whilst clocking up the years. Not a bad record by any standard. Being August, the weather protection sheet is stowed on the cab roof but come the winter, with its sleet, snow and cold winds, that cab does not seem like a good place to be especially working tender first! As an aside, the two cast irons plates attached to the shed wall inform interested parties that (top plate) 6in. S.V. [stop valve] 54ft connecting Felin Hen & column main. (lower plate) 8in. B.W.V. 53ft 6in. on column main. Local knowledge would know exactly what was what there but how many of those plates existed at engine sheds, and other railway installations which promulgated just local information - each one cast bespoke. *Ron Hodge.*

En route to its native LT&SR line, 3-cylinder Stanier Cl.4MT No.42520 called in at Kentish Town shed on 29th September 1955 after overhaul at Derby works. The whole class of thirty-seven engines was stationed on the London Tilbury & Southend section, allocated to three sheds - Plaistow, Shoeburyness and Tilbury. Other than visits to Bow works for minor repairs, the class attended Derby works for all major repairs. Amongst the LMS built 2-6-4Ts, this class was unique in having three cylinders as opposed to the normal two. However, the outside cylinders it will be noted were of a smaller diameter to the 2-cylinder engines at 16 inches against 19⅝ inches. Although largely confined to the LTS line during BR days, the class was more widely dispersed during LMS days, especially during WW2. The following sheds played hosts to various members of the class for differing periods of time from their introduction in 1934 to Nationalisation: Cricklewood, Derby, Heaton Mersey, Holbeck, Kentish Town, Kirkby-in-Ashfield, Leicester, Manningham, Millhouses, Newton Heath, Normanton, Nottingham, Saltley, Stourton, Trafford Park, Watford, and Willesden. Even BR tried them away from their natural habitat when Nos.42530 and 42535 were sent to the Scottish Region in the summer and winter of 1951 for trials on the Clyde coast commuter trains. They were allocated to Ardrossan, Corkerhill and Greenock either singly or as a pair during the period of residence. Both were back at Plaistow by April 1952. Withdrawals started in late 1960, a few more going in 1961 but the mass condemnation of June 1962 saw the class extinct. The lifelong theme of being different remained with this class right to the very end when many of them were sent to Doncaster works for scrapping. *Ron Hodge.*

Bristol Barrow Road shed towards the end when the surviving former Great Western engines in the Bristol area were welcomed for the last vestiges of steam workings then on offer. This former Midland roundhouse was a London Midland depot until February 1958 when it was gathered into the Western Region as British Railways began at last to tidy up the regional boundaries which had been created some ten years beforehand. This shed became 82E under the control of Bath Road shed, 82A. Its nearest neighbour to the north, at Barnwood in Gloucester, formerly 22B, became 85E under Worcester. Miraculously the allocations did not change because traffic patterns remained virtually unchanged so that Bristol based 'Jubilees' continued to work cross-country expresses as far as Sheffield and Leeds until steam motive power was eliminated on those services in favour of Type 4 diesel locomotives in the 1960s. This view of the shed yard circa 1964/65 shows not only a couple of newcomers but also a typical range of motive power which had inhabited this shed for the previous thirty years or so - 4F 0-6-0 No.44264, a Stanier Class 5 and a 'Jubilee' in the shape of by now nameless No.45608 (ex GIBRALTAR) from Holbeck. The BR Std. 9F is No.92051 whilst the WR proper is represented by what appears to be a 72XX 2-8-2T nosing into the roundhouse, and on the left of the shed an unidentified 'Castle' with a Collett straight sided tender. Their last GWR haven at St Philips March had closed in June 1964. The 'Jubilee' was withdrawn in September 1965 whilst the 4F went in November 1965. The 9F was a visitor from the north, more than likely Kirkby-in-Ashfield. The last members of the WR 72XX class were condemned in June 1965. Barrow Road shed closed for good in November 1965 when steam was totally obliterated in the Bristol area. Therefore, putting all those dates into a mix we can virtually conclude that we are viewing the shed yard as of late summer 1964 or spring/summer 1965 – the former gets my vote. On closure in 1965, as 82E, only three of the 4F 0-6-0s represented the old LMS contingent, the rest of the allocation was made up of orphan ex GWR types and a few BR Standards. *David Dalton.*